# KIM KARDASHIAN WEST

## AND

# KANYE WEST

POWER COUPLES™

# KIM KARDASHIAN WEST
## AND
# KANYE WEST

Monique Vescia

New York

Published in 2020 by The Rosen Publishing Group, Inc.
29 East 21st Street, New York, NY 10010

Copyright © 2020 by The Rosen Publishing Group, Inc.

First Edition

All rights reserved. No part of this book may be reproduced in any form without permission in writing from the publisher, except by a reviewer.

**Library of Congress Cataloging-in-Publication Data**

Names: Vescia, Monique, author.
Title: Kim Kardashian West and Kanye West / Monique Vescia.
Description: New York : Rosen Publishing, 2020. | Series: Power couples | Audience: Grades 7–12. | Includes bibliographical references and index.
Identifiers: LCCN 2018053776| ISBN 9781508188889 (library bound) | ISBN 9781508188872 (paperback)
Subjects: LCSH: Kardashian, Kim, 1980– —Juvenile literature. | West, Kanye—Juvenile literature.
Classification: LCC PN1992.4.A2 V47 2020 | DDC 782.421649092 [B]—dc23
LC record available at https://lccn.loc.gov/2018053776

*Manufactured in China*

**On the cover:** In May 2016, Kim Kardashian West and Kanye West attend the Manus x Machina: Fashion in an Age of Technology Costume Institute Gala at the Metropolitan Museum of Art in New York City.

# CONTENTS

**INTRODUCTION** ................................................. 6

CHAPTER 1
**RAISING KANYE** ............................................. 10

CHAPTER 2
**GROWING UP KARDASHIAN** ............................. 25

CHAPTER 3
**BECOMING KIMYE** ......................................... 39

CHAPTER 4
**JOINT ASSETS** .............................................. 48

CHAPTER 5
**COURTING CONTROVERSY AND TROUBLE** ........ 59

CHAPTER 6
**POLITICAL POWER COUPLE** ........................... 69

CHAPTER 7
**PLANS FOR WORLD DOMINATION** ................... 79

**TIMELINE** .................................................... 88
**GLOSSARY** ................................................... 90
**FOR MORE INFORMATION** ............................. 93
**FOR FURTHER READING** ................................ 97
**BIBLIOGRAPHY** ............................................ 98
**INDEX** ...................................................... 108

# INTRODUCTION

Over the top does not begin to describe it. The lavish rehearsal dinner took place in the mirrored Palace of Versailles, once home to French king Louis XVI and his wife, Marie Antoinette. Afterward, the wedding party boarded private planes and jetted off to Florence, Italy, for the ceremony, which was held in a sixteenth-century fortress, on May 24, 2014.

Italian tenor Andrea Bocelli sang "Ave Maria" as the bride walked up the aisle in a $500,000 Givenchy dress, trailing a white cathedral-length veil behind her. The couple recited their vows in front of a 26-foot (6-meter) wall created entirely from fragrant white flowers and nibbled bites of a seven-tier wedding cake. One photograph of the newly married couple sharing a kiss in front of the flower wall broke an internet record with nearly 2.5 million likes on Instagram.

It would be easy to mistake this ultraextravagant affair for a royal wedding, and in many ways that's exactly what it was. Megastars Kim Kardashian West and Kanye West function in American culture like members of the royal family. But unlike members of the British royalty, Kim and Kanye weren't born famous—they are self-created.

Kim Kardashian West, future reality TV star and business mogul, grew up in a wealthy Armenian

A-list newlyweds Kim and Kanye only have eyes for each other at the 2014 LACMA Art + Film Gala in Los Angeles, California.

American family in Beverly Hills, California. The brilliant and mercurial rap artist Kanye West, a man who once posed on the cover of *Rolling Stone* magazine wearing a crown of thorns, was raised by a single mother in a middle-class suburb of Chicago, Illinois.

Both Kardashian West and West used their energies, talents, and business instincts to become two of the most recognizable people on the planet, amassing fabulous wealth along the way. They have proved exceptionally adept at exploiting social media to enrich themselves and increase their fame. Yet despite these successes, each has suffered devastating loss, and weathered controversy and public humiliation.

When Kardashian West and West became "Kimye," they merged two separate business empires: the Kardashian TV-driven juggernaut and West's mastery of the hip-hop universe and entrepreneurial genius. The pairing made sense to many. The two seem to share the same goals, and neither has shied away from life in the public eye. Each of these megacelebrities is fully capable of breaking the internet all on their own. What might happen when they joined forces?

Two influential and highly compatible individuals working in tandem form a power couple: two people who accomplish even more as a team than they have achieved in their solo careers. Since their marriage, Kim and Kanye have dominated the spotlight, launching lucrative new businesses and doubling their influence over the most powerful people in the United States, including President Donald J. Trump. If West is serious about running for president himself, as he declared in 2018, these two might one day be living in the White House. Kanye West once compared their relationship to "two superheroes flying together." For this power couple, the sky's the limit.

CHAPTER 1

# RAISING KANYE

Hate him or love him, but chances are you've heard of Kanye West. From the very beginning, West set out to position himself in the red-hot bull's-eye of the public's attention. He has accomplished this goal by being as talented as he is outspoken.

## ORIGINS OF A HIP-HOP STAR

Kanye Omari West was born on June 8, 1977, in Atlanta, Georgia. His father, Ray, worked as a photojournalist. Donda West, Kanye's mother, was

Like mother, like son: Donda West beams with love and pride at the 2005 *Billboard* Music Awards, when Kanye took home the eighth annual Artist Achievement Award.

> Ray West's photojournalism helped expose economic injustice. Here a boy straddles a raw sewage ditch next to the Perry Homes housing projects (since demolished) in Atlanta, Georgia, in one of his photographs.

a teacher who earned her PhD and later became an English professor at Chicago State University.

Ray and Donda separated before Kanye was one and divorced when he was three, but the pair remained on friendly terms. After his parents' divorce, Kanye lived with his mother in Chicago's South Shore neighborhood during the school year, and he traveled back to Atlanta to spend the summers with his dad.

## THE COLOR OF MUSIC

Donda West had hundreds of records, and Kanye grew up in a house filled with music, even before he began making it himself. He claims he has a condition called synesthesia, which in his case means he visualizes sounds as specific colors: for instance, he perceives piano music as blue, and bass lines as dark brown and purple. From an early age, Kanye showed talent in both music and art, and Donda arranged for her son to have private lessons in both.

One of Kanye's first creative ambitions was to make video games. But he soon realized he liked composing the background music for the games more than making the games themselves.

## NURTURING A PRODIGY

Each parent had an influence on Kanye's development. Ray's photography and his involvement with the Black Panthers (an African American political organization) helped shape the person Kanye would become. He inherited his dad's artistic talent as well as Ray's willingness to stand up for what he believed in.

Donda West championed her son's ambitions from the very start. She bolstered Kanye's self-confidence and supported him from the earliest stages of his musical career. When he was thirteen years old, she took him to record his first rap song, "Green Eggs and Ham," in a basement studio.

## BUILDING A HOME STUDIO

At age fourteen, Kanye started saving up to buy his own electronic keyboard. As Donda West recalled, the model he had his eye on was a professional-quality instrument that cost $1,500. He managed to save $500, and for Christmas his mom gave him the rest of the money. Kanye holed up in his bedroom with the keyboard for hours, working on beats. After school, his friends would come over and they'd listen to Run DMC and Public Enemy and write beats together. Kanye took on part-time jobs so he could buy more equipment for his home studio, including a drum machine, a turntable, and a sound mixer. The only break from the pounding beats that shook the house came when Kanye went to a movie or played basketball with his friends. He poured his energies into his music, only leaving his room at mealtimes and to go to school. He told people he was going to be the best rapper in the world.

## A DIFFERENT PATH

Kanye attended Polaris High School in Oak Lawn, Illinois. He was an honors student before his obsession with music began to distract him from his classes and his grades started to slip. Still, it was obvious Kanye had artistic talent—he'd been entering (and winning) national art competitions since he was fourteen.

After graduation, he won a scholarship to study at Chicago's American Academy of Art. However, he left the program after a semester when his family could not afford the tuition and transferred to Chicago State, where Donda was on the faculty.

Kanye's parents took it hard when he eventually dropped out of school to make music full time. Years later, he memorialized that fateful decision in the title of his first album: *The College Dropout*.

## THE ROOTS OF RAP

Rap, the art of speaking rhyming lyrics, often over instrumental music, is an important element of hip-hop culture. Hip-hop was born in the Bronx, one of the five boroughs of New York City. The Bronx had a large population of African Americans and Latinos, and in the mid-1970s it had become an increasingly dangerous place. Landlords had let their properties fall into disrepair, and these abandoned buildings attracted criminal activity, such as drug-dealing, arson, and murder.

Blacks and Latinos living in the Bronx had few resources, yet they used what they had to invent new forms of self-expression and entertainment. Jamaican immigrant Clive Campbell, who called himself DJ Kool Herc, began organizing street parties and playing records on turntables for crowds that would gather. People loved dancing to the instrumental breaks in the music, so Herc started patching the breaks together by using the same record on two turntables and alternating between them. "B-boys" showed off their acrobatic moves during these extended breaks, and their routines became known as break dancing.

Other DJs followed Herc's lead and incorporated new sounds into the music, like scratching, created by moving a record back and forth across a phonograph needle to make a scratching sound. While the DJs coaxed sounds from the turntables, an MC (master

*(continued on the next page)*

*(continued from the previous page)*

of ceremonies) would keep the crowd whipped up. MCs started rhyming, or rapping, over the music, praising the DJ and boasting about their own rhyming ability. The best MCs attracted large crowds eager to hear their fast-paced wordplay. Hip-hop originated in the Bronx, but it eventually spread across the United States and beyond, spawning a rich culture of styles and traditions still relevant today.

## EARLY MUSICAL INFLUENCES

The Chicago hip-hop scene attracted Kanye. At age fifteen, he got to know a local DJ and music producer named No I.D., who became his mentor. In hip-hop music, the term "producer" means someone who creates the music that will be rapped over. Kanye (who today goes by Ye) was a quick study and began producing for local rap artists.

Kanye developed his own signature style, called chipmunk soul, which featured samples from soul tracks played at high speed. By creating surprising combinations of hard-pounding beats and smooth melodies, he built a unique sound. He started selling beats to other rap artists for $250 a track.

During this time, Kanye lived with his mother, paying her $200 every month. He didn't always

Guests at this 2011 hip-hop event in New York witnessed a warm reunion between West and producer No I.D., who once served as Ye's mentor and recognized his talents early on.

manage to sell enough beats to make his rent so he had to take on other jobs. At night, he worked on his music. In an interview with MTV in 2002, West described his ambitions and how his upbringing helped feed them: "I just had the hunger. My mother never raised me to ask for a handout."

I just had the hunger. My mother never raised me to ask for a handout."

—Kanye West

## BUILDING A REPUTATION

Chicago rapper Gravity (Grav) gave West his first big break. Kanye mixed beats for Grav's record, and earned $8,000 for one of his own beats, as Donda West recalled in the book she wrote about her son. In 1998, rapper Jermaine Dupri bought one of West's beats for his album *Life in 1472*, and the album went to number five on the *Billboard* 200 chart (a weekly ranking of the most popular albums in the United

## FRIENDS AND RIVALS

Shawn Corey Carter, also known as Jay-Z, is one of the world's best-selling music artists. After West was hired at Roc-A-Fella, a record label that Jay-Z had cofounded, his business relationship with Jay-Z evolved into a friendship. Unlike Kanye, Jay-Z grew up in Brooklyn, New York, and lived the rough life that rap often celebrates. In 2011, the two collaborated on a studio album called *Watch the Throne*, which topped the rap, pop, and R&B charts.

    The friendship turned soured when Jay-Z and his wife, the singer Beyoncé, skipped West's 2014 wedding to Kim Kardashian. Then the two friends clashed over a money dispute about TIDAL, Jay-Z's music-streaming service. The internet buzzed about their feud, but the pair has made efforts to mend their complicated relationship. In 2018, West tweeted that a sequel to *Watch the Throne* was "coming soon."

States). West also worked with Foxy Brown, Eminem, and Lil' Kim—all well-known rappers. Kanye West was making a name for himself as a talented and hardworking producer.

## ROC-A-FELLA DAYS

In 2000, West signed on as a producer at the Roc-A-Fella records label. Founded in 1996 by Shawn "Jay-Z" Carter, Kareem Burke, and Damon Dash, "The Roc" rose to dominate the New York rap scene. People often credit West's production work with making Jay-Z's 2001 album *The Blueprint* a success. But West's real ambition was to write his own music.

Damon Dash thought he might lose West as a producer if he didn't sign him as a rap artist, so he did—somewhat reluctantly. Kanye did not look like a typical rap musician. He wore pink polo shirts with turned-up collars

West and Roc-A-Fella cofounder Damon Dash are pictured here in 2002 at a New York party promoting Rocawear. The hip-hop clothing line has since generated hundreds of millions of dollars in revenue.

and Gucci loafers, and he came from a middle-class background. But Roc-A-Fella gave him a shot.

## A NEW LIFE, AND A BRUSH WITH DEATH

By 2000, West had saved enough money to move to New York, where he thought he'd have more opportunities than in Chicago. He found a place he could afford in nearby Newark, New Jersey, and got a job as a telemarketer, often staying up until 4 a.m. to work on his music.

On October 23, 2002, everything changed. While in Los Angeles, California, West fell asleep at

## KANYE STYLE

Calling himself the "Louis Vuitton Don," West flaunted luxury brands on stage and in his videos, and people started copying his preppy style, wearing polo shirts, argyle sweaters, and Louis Vuitton backpacks. During his 2008 Glow in the Dark tour, West wore "shutter" shades and sparked a huge trend: soon everyone was wearing a pair of the sunglasses with the thin slats across the lenses.

West had always been interested in fashion design and wanted to launch his own line, so in 2009, he interned at the Italian fashion brand Fendi, learning the business from the ground up.

the wheel and hit a car head-on, seriously injuring himself and another driver. In the hospital recovering from the accident, West had a revelation: instead of relying on the typical violent themes in rap, such as shootings and crime, he would rap about personal relationships, education, religion, and other experiences that had been important in his own life.

## THE TURNING POINT

After his release from the hospital, West recorded "Through the Wire," rapping with his broken jaw wired shut

West and Jamie Foxx perform "Slow Jamz" by the rapper Twista at the 2004 American Music Awards. West later left the event in anger when he failed to win an award.

as a result of the accident. This and other songs, such as "Jesus Walks," made up his first solo album, *The College Dropout* (2004).

The album marked a turning point in West's life and received high praise from music reviewers. According to Matt Green's book *The Amazing Life of Kanye West*, the record sold 440,000 copies right after its release and went platinum—selling a million copies in just eight weeks. That year, 2004, West earned ten Grammy nominations, including two for "Jesus Walks." He won for Best Rap Song and Best Rap Album. He also continued producing hit songs for headliners like Ludacris, Alicia Keys, Janet Jackson, Maroon 5, John Legend, and Beyoncé.

## BEHAVING BADLY

West also made headlines for his arrogance at the 2004 American Music Awards. He had been nominated for a Best New Artist Award but lost to the country music artist Gretchen Wilson. West stormed the stage and then left the auditorium in a huff, declaring he'd been robbed of the win. This incident wouldn't be the last time West's outrageous behavior made front-page news.

## SECOND TIME'S A CHARM

In 2004, West founded his own record label, G.O.O.D., which stood for Getting Out Our Dreams.

He followed up on the success of *The College Dropout* with his second album, *Late Registration*, in 2005. He wanted to keep pushing the envelope on what rap could sound like and the subjects it could address. This time he worked with a full orchestra and wrote music that highlighted social injustice, as in "Diamonds from Sierra Leone," about how the diamond trade devastated that West African country. Critics in *Time*, *Rolling Stone*, and *Spin* all raved about *Late Registration*, and it won a Grammy for Best Rap Album of 2005.

## HEARTBREAK

West was now making millions from his music. Donda West retired from her academic life to work as her son's manager. She wrote a book called *Raising Kanye: Life Lessons from the Mother of a Hip-Hop Superstar*.

Shortly after its publication in 2007, Donda West had cosmetic surgery. She went in for a breast reduction, tummy tuck, and liposuction and died the following day, possibly from complications from those procedures. She was only fifty-eight years old.

The sudden loss of his beloved mother devastated West. After her death, he broke up with his fiancée, fashion designer Alexis Phifer, and went to Hawaii for three weeks. There he recorded a pop album called *808s & Heartbreak*, filled with dark songs about pain and loneliness. ("808" refers to an electronic drum machine, the Roland TR-808.) For the vocals, West used Auto-Tune, an electronic pitch corrector that creates a disembodied, robotic sound. Many critics rank the record among West's best.

## THE MADNESS OF KING KANYE

After a two-year break from music, West made the record that many believe cemented his place in the pantheon of rap gods. *My Beautiful Dark Twisted Fantasy* (2010) received nearly unanimous praise from critics. *Rolling Stone* raved, "It's [West's] most maniacally inspired music yet. Nobody halfway sane could have made this album."

CHAPTER 2

# GROWING UP KARDASHIAN

Kanye West's life as a cherished only child from a middle-class home was very different from being raised as part of a lively and blended household, surrounded by siblings, in a wealthy neighborhood. That environment helped shape the ambitious little girl who transformed herself into one of the most famous brands on Earth.

## A BEVERLY HILLS CHILDHOOD

Imagine growing up in a sun-drenched world of wealth and privilege, surrounded by talk show hosts and rock stars. Kimberly Noel Kardashian entered

# KIM KARDASHIAN WEST AND KANYE WEST

> Kim Kardashian's Buckley School picture from kindergarten, in 1984, shows that the future reality TV star and beauty mogul knew how to accessorize from an early age.

this world on October 21, 1980, the second of four children born to Robert and Kris Kardashian. Kourtney, Kim, and their younger siblings, Khloé and Robert Jr. (called Rob), lived in a large house on the private cul-de-sac of Tower Lane in Beverly Hills, California. The estate boasted a tennis court, a Jacuzzi, and a swimming pool. Robert and Kris loved throwing lavish parties. Some of the famous people who owned property nearby included talk show host Jay Leno and musician Bruce Springsteen.

When she was little, Kim shared a room with her older sister, Kourtney, though the family mansion had enough bedrooms for everyone. Just two years apart, the two sisters were close and would wear matching outfits, so people sometimes mistook them for twins. Kim was a sweet and pretty child, whose father nicknamed her Kimbo. She was short, with dark hair and big dark eyes, like her mother and

## THE SIMPLE LIFE

Between 2004 and 2007, Paris Hilton, heiress to the Hilton hotel chain, and her socialite friend Nicole Richie starred in a reality television show. Various episodes featured them "working" at different low-paying jobs and generally creating problems for their noncelebrity hosts and employers. Viewers got to know Paris's childhood friend Kim Kardashian, who appeared on the show from time to time. Both Kardashian and Hilton worked hard to attract media attention and keep the spotlight on themselves. But Kardashian's fame quickly eclipsed Hilton's, in part because Kim proved so adept at exploiting the new possibilities of social media.

father. Kim went to preschool with Paris Hilton, whose great-grandfather founded the Hilton chain of hotels. Kim and Paris became best friends.

## THE ARMENIAN AMERICAN DREAM

The family's Armenian heritage was an essential part of life in the Kardashian home. Kim's great-grandparents immigrated to the United States from Karakale, Armenia, in 1913. They worked hard to establish themselves in their new home and eventually made millions in the meatpacking business. However, some of their business practices caught the attention of the Federal Bureau of Investigation (FBI), and Robert's brother, Tom, was charged with bribing federal meat inspectors. President George H. W. Bush later granted him a pardon.

Unlike his brother, Robert Kardashian didn't go into the family business. Instead, he earned a business degree and founded Movie Tunes, Inc., a music and marketing company. He also attended law school and became a prominent attorney. But he never let his children forget their Armenian roots.

Kim grew up eating Armenian food at home and celebrating Armenian holidays. Sometimes Armenian immigrants in the United States dropped the "-ian" from their names, for fear of being identified as Armenian. But Kim's dad was proud of his heritage and made his daughters promise that they would never change their last names.

## WHERE ON EARTH IS ARMENIA?

Armenia shares a border with Turkey, Iran, Azerbaijan, and Georgia on the continent of Asia. In 2016, it had a population of three million people, one-third the population of New York City. Armenian immigrants began arriving in California in the early twentieth century, fleeing unrest, religious persecution, and poverty in their homeland. The Los Angeles suburb of Glendale, California, is now home to the largest Armenian population in the West. Armenian surnames typically end with "-ian." Like the "-son" at the end of the surname Anderson, the suffix indicates a family relationship. "Kardashian" means "from the family or clan of Kardash."

## A CHRISTIAN HOME

Robert Kardashian was a born-again Christian who read the Bible every day. The family said grace before every meal and listened to gospel music at home. They always attended church on Sundays. The kids attended private Catholic schools, although the Kardashians were not Catholic. Kris and Robert approved of the school's strict rules and high academic standards.

## TROUBLE IN PARADISE

When Kim turned ten, her idyllic life was shattered. That year, her parents told the kids that they planned to file for divorce. Kris Kardashian had been having a secret romantic affair with a soccer player named Todd Waterman, and she wanted out of the marriage. Their parents' divorce came as a shock to the Kardashian children, who didn't remember their parents fighting.

In 1991, a month after the divorce became final, Kris married the Olympic athlete Bruce Jenner. Kim and her siblings now belonged to a large blended family that would eventually include Bruce's four kids from his two previous marriages and his two daughters with Kris, Kendall and Kylie. (Kris and Bruce's marriage would last for twenty-two years, until they split and Bruce transitioned from male to female, becoming Caitlyn.)

The telegenic Kardashian-Jenner clan poses for a family portrait in 1991. Kim (*at right*) once said that "having lots of siblings is like having built-in best friends."

# GROWING UP KARDASHIAN

This yearbook photograph from 1997 is from Kim's junior year. Kim graduated from Marymount High School in Los Angeles in 1998. She attended her twenty-year reunion there in 2018.

Kim got along well with her stepfather, Bruce. After the divorce, Kris and Robert maintained an amicable relationship.

## A POPULAR GIRL

In 1994, Kim began attending Marymount High School, an exclusive girls' school in Bel-Air, a ritzy neighborhood in western Los Angeles. She was a good student and active in various school clubs. Like her siblings, Kim was popular in school, although she suffered teasing when she began to develop physically. Kim now celebrates her curvaceous body, but in *Kardashian Konfidential* she admits that when she was young she often prayed to God to stop her breasts from growing.

31

## THE TRIAL OF THE CENTURY

As a close friend of former Hall of Fame football player and actor O. J. Simpson, Robert Kardashian became a household name. On June 12, 1994, O. J. Simpson's former wife, Nicole Brown Simpson, and her friend Ronald Goldman were found stabbed to death on the steps of her home. Charged with their murders, Simpson went on the run. Hours of live TV footage of a white Ford Bronco driving slowly down the Los Angeles freeways transfixed the nation. When the low-speed car chase finally ended and detectives took Simpson into custody, they retrieved a bag containing his passport, along with several disguises, $8,000 in cash, and a loaded gun.

Robert Kardashian served as a member of the legal "dream team" that defended Simpson during the 1995 trial that obsessed American viewers for eight months. An estimated one hundred million people tuned in to watch the reading of the verdict on live TV, and many white people were shocked to see black people jubilantly celebrating Simpson's acquittal. The so-called trial of the century revealed the complexity of race relations in the United States. According to the *Washington Post*, in 1997, 82 percent of whites believed Simpson (who is African American) was guilty, while only 31 percent of blacks did.

Robert Kardashian's (*center*) role as a member of the defense team during the televised O. J. Simpson murder trial in 1995 helped introduce the public to the Kardashian name.

The trial also split the Kardashian household: Kris believed O. J. was a murderer, while Robert staunchly supported his best friend and former business partner. (Later, he came to doubt his friend's innocence.) Ironically, Kardashian hated the media attention that his own involvement in the trial brought to his former wife and daughters.

## LOVES AND LOSSES

In high school, Kim dated T. J. Jackson, the nephew of pop superstar Michael Jackson. She celebrated her fourteenth birthday with T. J. and a group of her friends at Jackson's Neverland Ranch, where they went on amusement park rides and saw baby elephants and chimps wearing overalls.

Kim and T. J. dated for over a year, and they attended Kim's high school prom together. Tragedy brought them even closer. In 1994, T. J. lost his mother, Dee Dee (Delores), when she was found dead in a swimming pool. Dee Dee's boyfriend was later convicted of her murder.

In 2000, when she was nineteen, Kim Kardashian eloped with music producer Damon Thomas. The pair split after four years together. In court papers filed during their divorce, Kardashian claimed Thomas abused her during their marriage.

## A FATHER'S LEGACY

Robert Kardashian enjoyed being involved in his children's lives. In *Kardashian Konfidential*, Kim and her sisters recall how every night around the dinner table, they took part in a family ritual called "the pit and the peak," when Robert asked everyone to share the high and low points of their day.

Kardashian believed his children should learn to work hard and use their own abilities to achieve success in life, rather than relying on family wealth. On her sixteenth birthday, Kim was given a brand-new white BMW. "My dad made me sign a contract … that if I hit my car I would be responsible for paying for it," Kim explains in *Kardashian Konfidential*. Kim and her siblings all knew that when they turned eighteen, they could no longer count on financial support from their parents.

In July 2003, Robert Kardashian was diagnosed with esophageal cancer. Kourtney and Kim stayed by their father's side in those final weeks of his illness and death, at the age of fifty-nine. The loss devastated his family. In his 2017 biography *The Kardashians: An American Drama*, Jerry Oppenheimer writes that Robert Kardashian claimed a prophetess told him that the Kardashian name would one day be world famous. Unfortunately, he did not live long enough to see that prophecy come true.

## A SEVENTY-TWO-DAY MARRIAGE

Kim's romances with various male celebrities raised her visibility in the public eye. Kardashian dated Nick Lachey, a former member of the boy band 98 Degrees. Kardashian was also involved with Reggie Bush, a former running back for the New Orleans Saints. In 2011, Kardashian became engaged to pro basketball player Kris Humphries. Their lavish wedding cost $20 million and aired as a four-part special on the E! network. But during the honeymoon,

Kardashian realized she'd made a mistake. The couple filed for divorce seventy-two days later.

## A NEW FAMILY BUSINESS

In the years after their father's death, Kim, Kourtney, and Khloé had discussed collaborating on a business venture. They liked the idea of a project they could work on together as sisters. In 2006, they opened DASH, a clothing and accessories store, in Calabasas, California. For a time,

In 2006, Kim, Khloé, and Kourtney Kardashian (*left to right*) started the DASH boutique as a family project. In 2018, the clothing and accessory chain closed its doors.

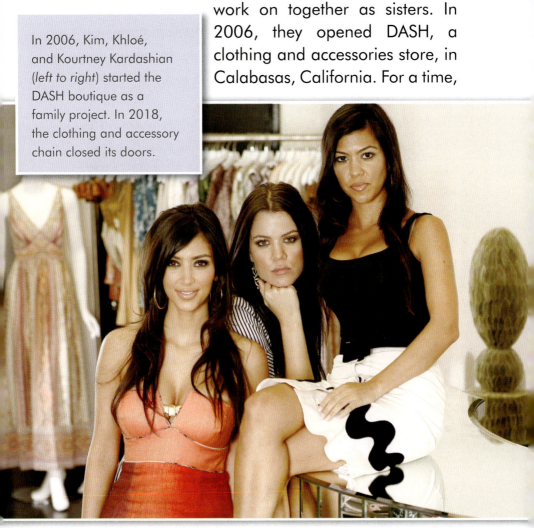

all three worked together in the store, struggling to pay the bills. The store failed to turn a profit for many years, but eventually the business did well enough that the Kardashians were able to open additional DASH stores in New York City and Miami, Florida.

## MODERN-DAY BRADY BUNCH

The Jenner-Kardashian household was a lively place, full of laughter and good-natured arguments. A close friend, Kathie Lee Gifford, always found these gatherings highly entertaining. Gifford, a popular talk-show host, thought the family deserved to have its own television show.

In *Kardashian Konfidential*, Kim confesses, "I always wanted to be a reality TV star." So-called reality TV shows, in which a television crew films a group of nonactors going about their daily lives, had proved to be a moneymaker for many networks. Shows such as MTV's *The Real World* and *Big Brother* were cheap to produce and attracted large audiences.

Ryan Seacrest, host of the singing competition *American Idol*, had been looking for a family to build a reality show around for his own production company. He dispatched a videographer to the Kardashian-Jenner house to film a family barbecue.

> **I always wanted to be a reality TV star."**
> **—KIM KARDASHIAN**

# KIM KARDASHIAN WEST AND KANYE WEST

The producers of *Keeping Up with the Kardashians* came up with the show's name when one of them complained that she had trouble matching the pace of the energetic family.

As Seacrest told *Haute Living* magazine, the cameraman later called to rave, "It's absolutely golden. You're going to die when you see this tape." Seacrest thought viewers would love the crazy, fun-loving, telegenic family. *Keeping Up with the Kardashians* premiered on October 14, 2007, and would become one of the longest-running reality series. By 2016, according to *Forbes*, the Kardashian-Jenner empire had a net worth of $122.5 million.

CHAPTER 3

# BECOMING KIMYE

When the news dropped that Kim Kardashian and Kanye West had officially become an item, plenty of people weren't terribly surprised. To many observers, the "Kimye" (as many call them) matchup made a lot of sense.

In addition to being individuals with narcissistic tendencies who crave the spotlight, the two have a lot in common. They both grew up in Christian households, and each experienced the sudden loss of a beloved parent relatively early in life. Family

# KIM KARDASHIAN WEST AND KANYE WEST

Kim Kardashian attends a 2009 New York fashion show with running back Reggie Bush (*far right*). Kanye West (*second from left*) and Kardashian were good friends before they began dating.

is important to them both, and Kanye received a warm welcome from the Kardashian-Jenner clan.

## A FASHIONABLE PAIR

Kim Kardashian had started out as a fashion stylist and opened a chain of clothing stores with her sisters, and West's designs had been shown at Fashion Week in Paris, France, and New York City. The two appeared together in the front-row seats at fashion shows, watching models walk the runway in the latest styles. Finally, both had proved successful at using their talents to make vast amounts of money.

# KANYE RAPS ABOUT KIM

Kanye West's decision to rap about his own feelings and experiences rather than the typical themes of rap was key to his success as an artist. Over the years, West never hid his growing feelings for Kim Kardashian, and he made many references to her in his music, often in not safe (or suitable) for work (NSFW) lyrics. Listeners heard references to Kim in "Knock You Down" (2009), where he calls her "the cheerleader of my dreams," as well as in "Clique" and "Cold" from 2012, and "Drunk in Love" (2014). In the 2014 rap song "I Won," West refers to Kardashian as "the number one trophy wife."

West has been outspoken about his instant attraction to Kardashian. Besides being physically drawn to each other, over the years the two had developed a friendship.

> "I feel like the type of girl I would be with is a fellow superhero."
> —KANYE WEST

## HOW IT HAPPENED

Various online magazines report that Kanye once told *Details* in 2009, "I feel like the type of girl I would be with is a fellow superhero." The pairing of Kim Kardashian and Kanye West may have seemed to many like a match made in heaven, but it took a while for the stars to align. In the celebrity-verse, their paths would occasionally cross, but Kardashian was either married or dating other guys. In 2008, West hired her to appear in a racy hip-hop puppet show called *Alligator Boots*. She played the part of Princess Leia from *Star Wars*, wearing her slave outfit. West dressed as a storm trooper in glossy white armor. The two had undeniable chemistry, but the show didn't end up going anywhere.

In 2011, West made an appearance on *Kourtney and Kim Take New York*, a spin-off of *Keeping Up with the Kardashians (KUWTK)*. The sisters had opened a new DASH store in Manhattan, and West stopped by on camera. Kim said, "Kanye and I have been good friends for a long time … [W]e definitely respect his fashion taste and his style and so we wanted him to check out the store."

Before Kardashian married basketball player Kris Humphries in 2011, West tried to talk her out of tying the knot. As he admitted on the talk show *Kocktails with Khloé*, he'd never had a cell phone, but he bought one so he could send Kardashian unflattering pictures of basketball players with the comment "This is your future." Luckily for West, Kardashian's marriage to Humphries was extremely short-lived.

Finally, in the spring of 2012, people spotted the pair stepping out together, and their relationship became a public obsession. In addition to being a rap star, West had begun to establish a reputation as a fashion designer. In fact, he told the fashion magazine *Complex*, "I always say I was a designer before I was a rapper." West made an appearance in an episode of *KUWTK,* in which he and his personal stylist purged Kim's closet, tossing out some of her favorite shoes. Fans of the show called him controlling and expressed outrage about the episode, but others credit West with helping Kardashian project a more refined, luxe, and ultracool image. The pair became style icons, and often coordinated their outfits, favoring a neutral color palette of black, white, and beige.

## NORTH STAR

In December 2012, word splashed across the news that West and Kardashian were expecting a baby together. At the time, Kardashian was still legally married to Kris Humphries, although the couple had been living apart for more than a year. Kardashian

Kardashian and West are seen here at the 2013 Metropolitan Museum of Art's annual Costume Institute Gala. Kardashian, who was pregnant at the time, got slammed on social media for her choice of dress.

worried that she might still be married to Humphries when her daughter by West was born. At last, in April 2013, the divorce was finalized.

Before North West was born, five weeks premature, on June 15, 2013, Kim bought several strollers to be sure one would match her daughter's skin tone. The new parents brought their twenty-two-month-old daughter to Jerusalem to be baptized in a twelfth-century Armenian church in the ancient walled city. Nicknamed Nori, the child has been lavished with designer clothes and accessories since the day she was born.

## #WORLDSMOSTTALKEDABOUTCOUPLE

On October 21, 2013, Kardashian's thirty-third birthday, she and West became engaged. West's proposal took place at San Francisco's AT&T Park, a baseball stadium West had rented for the occasion. The park's Jumbotron flashed the message PLEEESE MARRY MEEE!!! when West took a knee and popped the question. When Kardashian said yes, her friends and family rushed to congratulate the couple and ogle the fifteen-carat diamond ring that West had given her. The news quickly went viral on the internet.

In the months before their wedding, West and Kardashian posed for the cover of the April 2014 issue of *Vogue*. In the photo, by renowned photographer Annie Leibovitz, Kardashian wears a cream-colored strapless gown, while West embraces her. The decision

## FIVE THINGS YOU PROBABLY DIDN'T KNOW ABOUT THE KIMYE WEDDING

The following details about the couple's wedding have not been widely reported:

1. The couple wanted to hold the actual wedding ceremony at the palace of Versailles, but permission was denied.
2. With the exception of a single official wedding photographer, no cameras were allowed at the ceremony.
3. Kardashian and her late father, Robert, loved the Italian tenor Andrea Bocelli. As Kardashian walked down the aisle on Caitlyn Jenner's arm, she thought the music she was hearing was a recording of Bocelli until she realized that the singer himself was serenading her.
4. Kim's sisters Kourtney and Khloé served as bridesmaids and they wore white dresses.
5. The groom's gift to the bride was a risqué portrait of her painted by the artist Bambi.

to put the couple on the cover offended some readers, who threatened to boycott the venerable fashion magazine. According to *USA Today*, Anna Wintour defended the decision in her April 2014 editor's letter, calling West a "cultural provocateur" who deserved to be featured, and saying that Kardashian, "through her strength of character, has created a place for herself in the glare of the world's spotlight, and it takes real guts to do that."

## JUST AN INTIMATE LITTLE AFFAIR

Although Kardashian told Ryan Seacrest on his KIIS FM radio show that she and Kanye wanted a "super, super-small intimate wedding," the event turned out to be anything but. The two hundred lucky A-listers on the guest list first gathered at the opulent palace of Versailles outside Paris for a rehearsal dinner and a private tour of the vast estate, capped off by a

This photograph shows a bird's-eye view of the Forte di Belvedere in Florence, Italy, where the Wests got married. Bernardo Buontalenti, the man who designed this fortress, purportedly invented Italian ice cream, or gelato, in 1565.

performance by singer Lana Del Ray. Reportedly, each guest received a security detail, luxurious spa treatments, and a private cell phone so no details about the event could be leaked. Then they all boarded private planes and flew to Italy for the ceremony the next day.

On May 24, 2014, Kim Kardashian and Kanye West were married at the Forte di Belvedere in Florence, Italy. The four-course reception dinner was served at a 224-foot (68-meter) imperial marble table, with each guest's name carved into its surface. In addition to the Kardashian-Jenner clan, attendees included singer John Legend and Chrissy Teigen, tennis star Serena Williams, rapper Jaden Smith (who came dressed as Batman), the rapper and actor Q-Tip, and former Chicago Bulls player Scottie Pippen. West's friend Jay-Z and his famous wife, Beyoncé, skipped the wedding.

## THE K-TEAM

Well-known married couples who live their lives under constant public scrutiny experience difficulties and challenges that other couples do not. Although only time will tell whether this particular marriage will last, the power duo's outsize ambitions appear to be in sync, and they seem fully supportive of each other's endeavors. It's also clear they have big plans for the future.

## CHAPTER 4

# JOINT ASSETS

The West-Kardashian wedding represented the merger of two of the world's most famous people, a union that the *New York Times* called "a historic blizzard of celebrity." Separately, they had become household names and earned millions of dollars. As a team, they attracted an even larger audience of avid fans, eager to follow them on Instagram, to copy their workouts, and to obsess over the smallest details of their fabulous lives. Now that they were officially a power couple, what would they do with all that power?

## BREAKING THE INTERNET

One of the first things that Kim Kardashian West (as she calls herself) did was "break" the internet. She posed for the winter 2014 issue of *Paper* magazine wearing practically nothing. The playful, NSFW cover had the tagline "Break the Internet," and suddenly all the social networking platforms and news outlets were buzzing about it.

## RACKING UP HONORS

While his wife was making jaws drop all over the world, Kanye West was adding to his growing pile of honors and awards. The men's fashion magazine

Kanye West looks very happy at the 2015 BET Honors award ceremony in Washington, DC. Accepting that year's Visionary Award, West gave a heartfelt speech about racism.

*GQ* honored him with the title "Most Stylist Man of the Year" in 2014 and again in 2015.

West's success in the fashion world has been due, in part, to his acclaimed wife. As he told *In Style* magazine, "She improved my style, we improved each other." In 2015, West and Kardashian West appeared together in a steamy ad campaign for the French luxury fashion brand Balmain. At that year's Metropolitan Museum of Art's gala, the pair rocked the red carpet with their glamorous and edgy looks.

## BEST FOOT FORWARD

Besides being a declaration of love and commitment, the Kardashian-West nuptials represented a powerful style statement, with the perfectionist West fussing over every detail, as he admitted to *GQ*. He had begun to earn respect as a fashion designer. Successful team-ups with Nike and Louis Vuitton to design athletic shoes were followed by a lucrative deal with Adidas that West inked at the end of 2013. In 2014, he put his music on hold to devote his energies to his Yeezy footwear designs, which he produces in collaboration with Adidas.

> "She improved my style, we improved each other."
> —KANYE WEST

West has proven incredibly masterful at building up the hype around his designs. Fans waited on the street for hours in the rain just to get a raffle ticket for a chance to get their hands on a pair of the

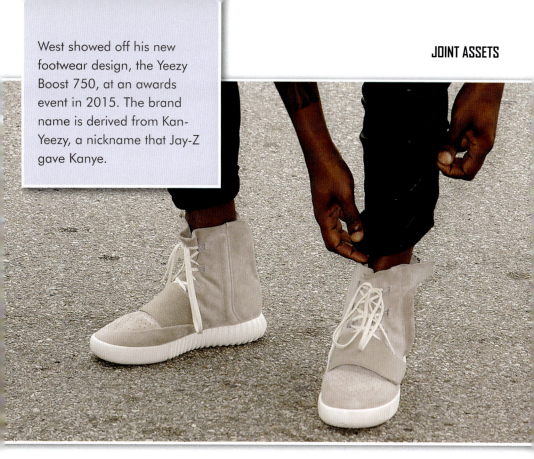

West showed off his new footwear design, the Yeezy Boost 750, at an awards event in 2015. The brand name is derived from Kan-Yeezy, a nickname that Jay-Z gave Kanye.

Yeezy Boost 350 Blacks. The Yeezy brand today sells apparel, footwear, and jewelry.

## MAKING BANK

By 2015, Yahoo! Finance reported that Kanye West's net worth was $145 million—not bad for a college dropout. According to *Forbes*, Kim Kardashian West's 2015 net income—including *KUWTK* and book royalties, profits from name and image licensing, and app and website earnings—amounted to $52.5 million, almost double her 2014 earnings. Both West and Kardashian West had proved that they could make it rain money.

## HIP-HOP FASHION MOGULS

Since the early 1970s, hip-hop culture has influenced fashion, first popularizing clothing such as Kangol hats, Puma sneakers, and Adidas track suits worn onstage by popular rappers Run DMC. Later, hip-hop stars adopted classic American brands such as Ralph Lauren and Tommy Hilfiger and luxury designers such as Gucci, Prada, and Versace. Because many rap stars grew up in low-income neighborhoods, wearing expensive designer clothes was a way to flaunt their new wealth and rising social status.

Eventually, rap artists saw there was serious money to be made in fashion design. Sean "Diddy" Combs transitioned from musician to mainstream fashion mogul with his Sean John fashion line. Grammy-winning artist Pharrell Williams has made millions from his high-end streetwear companies Billionaire Boys Club and Ice Cream. Roc-A-Fella record label's cofounders Jay-Z and Damon Dash founded the Rocawear fashion brand in 1999, which they sold in 2007 for $204 million in cash. Now, rap stars such as Cardi B, Jay-Z, and Nicki Minaj rub elbows with fashion editors in the coveted front-row seats at runway shows.

## PAYING IT FORWARD

The two didn't just spend their wealth on luxuries such as a Swarovski-crystal-encrusted rocking horse for

# JOINT ASSETS

> In 2010, Kim Kardashian brought her star power to a celebrity event benefiting the Dian Fossey Gorilla Fund International. She contributes both her time and money to many causes and charitable organizations.

North (oh, yes, they did). They also donated both time and money to some worthy causes.

Soles4Souls supplies footwear to victims of natural disasters. After hearing about a teen who was collecting shoes for a charity founded after the tsunami that devastated Indonesia in 2004, Kim and Kanye donated one thousand pairs of shoes to help her reach her goal.

Kardashian West regularly sells pieces she has worn or used, such as clothing or handbags, on the online auction site eBay. She donates a portion of the profits to organizations doing work that she believes in, such as the VOUS Church in Miami, Florida, which ministers to young adults.

After a friend's child got sick and was admitted to Children's Hospital in Los Angeles, Kardashian West began regularly visiting kids being treated there. She has also donated some of the profits from her eBay sales to the hospital.

## MORE HONORS

Each year since 2008, the BET network has celebrated Black History Month (in February) by recognizing the achievements of African Americans. In 2015, Kanye West won the BET Visionary Award. Damon Dash, one of the cofounders of the Roc-A-Fella label, presented West with the honor.

## MOST INFLUENTIAL COUPLE

In its annual issue celebrating the world's most influential people, *Time* magazine chooses one hundred names to feature. According to the magazine's criteria, the people who make the list are those who "one way or another … embody a breakthrough: they broke the rules, broke the record, broke the silence, broke the boundaries to reveal what we're capable of."

For the 2015 issue of *Time* 100, the editors chose both Kanye West and Kim Kardashian West. In the issue, Elon Musk, chief executive officer (CEO) of Tesla and SpaceX and a provocateur in his own right, calls West "a pop-culture juggernaut." He goes on to say, "Kanye's been playing the long game all along. We're only just beginning to see why." Kardashian West's profile calls her "the first lady of #fame" and a "media phenomenon."

Making the *Time* 100 list positioned the couple alongside some of the most prominent and powerful people on Earth. Others on the 2015 list include ballerina Misty Copeland, designer Alexander Wang, CEO of Apple Inc. Tim Cook, actress Julianne Moore, politician Hillary Clinton, Russian president Vladimir Putin, and leader of the Roman Catholic Church Pope Francis.

## GRADUATION DAY

On May 11, 2015, something happened to Kanye West that would have made his late mother, Professor Donda West, extremely proud. Beaming in his long black robe, the former college

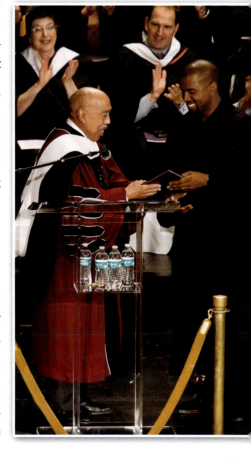

Kanye receives an honorary PhD at the School of Art Institute of Chicago. The school's decision to award a doctorate to West proved to be a controversial one.

dropout received an honorary PhD from the School of the Art Institute of Chicago. Sometimes colleges and universities will award an academic degree to someone who did not officially attend the school but who nonetheless has made an important contribution to the world.

## THE QUEEN OF SELFIES

Did you know that June 21 is National Selfie Day? Photographic self-portraits have become a common way of documenting one's life. Kim Kardashian West raised the selfie to an art form when she published *Selfish,* a 448-page coffee table book featuring photographs she'd taken of herself. *Selfish* documents nine years of Kardashian West's life.

Not everyone approved of the reality star's unabashed objectification of her own beauty. Tim Gunn of *Project Runway* fame lamented to *US* magazine, "What if this is the only thing that survives in the time capsule? I feel my IQ plummeting." Other reviewers were more positive, and saw the book as an ode to the hard work (and the army of personal stylists) that such beauty requires. Following its publication in May 2015, *Selfish* became a *New York Times* best-seller. Revised and expanded editions came out in 2016 and 2017.

## WHAT IS A SURROGATE?

In a process called in vitro fertilization (IVF), an egg is harvested from a mother and fertilized with a father's sperm. Then the fertilized egg is implanted in the uterus of a surrogate (substitute) mother. The surrogate mother hired by Kim and Kanye for their third child received $45,000, according to *Vogue* in March 2018, and had to refrain from doing anything that might hurt the unborn baby, such as drinking, smoking or taking drugs, or even using hair dye. West and Kardashian West were both present in the delivery room when the baby was born. Other celebrity couples who have used surrogates include actors Sarah Jessica Parker and Matthew Broderick and Angela Bassett and Courtney B. Vance.

## GROWING A FAMILY, ONE WAY OR ANOTHER

West and Kardashian West welcomed a second child into the world at the end of 2015, when their son, Saint West, was born on December 5. As with her first child, Kim experienced complications during the pregnancy, including preeclampsia, a potentially dangerous condition characterized by high blood pressure.

After her daughter North's delivery, Kardashian West had suffered another serious complication called placenta accreta. In most cases, the placenta (the organ that nourishes the fetus before birth) will be naturally expelled from the mother's womb after the baby is delivered. When it grows too deeply into the wall of the uterus, part or all of the placenta can remain attached. This complication can cause severe blood loss after delivery, endangering the mother's life. After North's birth, Kardashian West had two operations to remove the remaining placenta and scar tissue from her uterus.

After Saint's delivery, Kardashian West underwent surgery to repair a hole in her uterus. Afterward, the doctor warned her that it would be risky for her to carry another pregnancy to term. The couple wanted another child, so they opted to use a surrogate. On January 15, 2018, they welcomed their second daughter, Chicago "Chi" West. In January 2019, the couple confirmed that they were expecting their fourth child, a boy, by surrogate.

## IN THE PUBLIC EYE

Some celebrities choose to shield their children from the media, never allowing their photographs to be made public. However, Kardashian West and West have proudly shared images of their kids via social media since the day they were born. Their growing family has clearly brought the power couple much joy, but maintaining such a high profile has its dangers, as they would soon learn.

# COURTING CONTROVERSY AND TROUBLE

Kim Kardashian West and Kanye West generate a media frenzy wherever they go. As a couple, they have had to beef up their own security details, hiring more people to protect them and their growing family twenty-four hours a day. Because Kardashian West was afraid the children might be kidnapped, she and her husband purchased a fleet of armored SUVs, which can supposedly withstand a landmine blast or a rocket-launched grenade.

## THE COST OF FAME

The need for security became apparent in October 2016, when masked thieves broke into her Paris hotel room and robbed Kardashian West at gunpoint. The robbers bound her with zip-ties and duct-taped her mouth, escaping with $10 million in jewelry (including her fifteen-carat engagement ring) and a Rolex. Though physically unhurt, the reality star was deeply shaken by the traumatic experience.

Kanye West interrupted a concert appearance, citing "a family emergency," and rushed to join his wife in Paris. After Kim's ordeal, the entire Kardashian-Jenner clan scaled back on public appearances. Filming on *Keeping Up with the Kardashians* was halted for three weeks. Kardashian West believes the perpetrators may have tracked her movements on Instagram, so after the incident she took a long break from social media. She also cancelled her scheduled public appearances, and the couple had a state-of-the-art panic room installed in their house.

## GETTING PHYSICAL

Kanye West has not always responded graciously to the swarms of paparazzi that mob him whenever he appears in public. In 2016, a photographer named Daniel Ramos filed a lawsuit against West. Ramos claimed that in July 2013, while he photographed the rap star at the Los Angeles International Airport,

West attacked him and tried to wrestle the camera out of his hands. West ultimately settled the case. He agreed to pay damages, and the judge fined Kanye two hundred hours of community service and ordered him to attend anger management classes.

## NO FILTER

West will be the first to tell you how amazingly talented he is, comparing himself to cultural icons such as Pablo Picasso, Steve Jobs, and Jimi Hendrix. His egotism is part of his public persona. His fans love that he is unfiltered and honest, but sometimes that bluntness has gotten him into trouble.

## AN AMERICAN TRAGEDY

One such event happened in the aftermath of Hurricane Katrina. In August 2005, a powerful tropical storm overwhelmed the US Gulf Coast, eventually flooding 80 percent of the city of New Orleans, Louisiana. Tens of thousands of residents, many of them African Americans from low-income neighborhoods, sought refuge on rooftops, in the sweltering Superdome sports stadium, and in the city's convention center. Poorly coordinated rescue attempts, insufficient medical care, water, and food, and a lack of basic sanitation all contributed to the deaths of more than 1,800 people from Katrina in the United States, according to the National Hurricane Center.

## STORM OF CONTROVERSY

On live television during "A Concert for Hurricane Relief" on September 2, 2005, Kanye West said something people would never forget. Scheduled to benefit the victims of Katrina, the charity telethon featured a star-studded lineup of actors and musicians donating their talents. West stood shoulder to shoulder with comedian Mike Myers, reading words off a teleprompter. But West went off script, insisting the federal response had been

After writing "Kanye West" on the neckline, bassist Flea of the Red Hot Chili Peppers donated his favorite T-shirt to an auction benefiting the victims of Hurricane Katrina.

# COURTING CONTROVERSY AND TROUBLE

slow because the majority of people suffering were African American. Then West uttered seven of the most unforgettable words ever spoken on live TV: "George Bush doesn't care about black people."

## DAMAGE CONTROL

West's claim horrified the show's producers, who moved quickly to contain the fallout. But musicians Harry Connick Jr. (a New Orleans native), and country singers Faith Hill and Tim McGraw approached Rick Kaplan, the show's executive producer, insisting that West was right. They had been to New Orleans and witnessed the inadequate federal response, and they agreed with Kanye.

The top executives at NBC would later edit those controversial remarks out of the broadcast, but many admired West's willingness to call it as he saw it. George Bush later told NBC's Matt Lauer that it was one of the lowest points of his presidency.

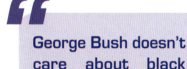

"George Bush doesn't care about black people."
—KANYE WEST

## STAGE BOMB

West has never been one to keep silent when he sees an injustice done. During the 2009 Video Music Awards (VMA), broadcast on MTV, singer Taylor Swift had just stepped up to accept her award for Best Female Video, when West bounded onstage

## KIM KARDASHIAN WEST AND KANYE WEST

> West angered Taylor Swift's fans when he grabbed the microphone from her during her acceptance speech at the VMAs. This impulsive act ignited an extended public feud between the two music artists.

and snatched the mic from her hands, shouting, "Sorry, Taylor, I'm really happy for you, and I'm-a let you finish, but Beyoncé had one of the best videos of all time!" West later apologized to Swift for interrupting her acceptance speech.

In the years that followed, residual bad feelings between West and Swift would bubble up into a public spat featuring veiled and not-so-veiled references in their song lyrics. Kim Kardashian West entered the fray as well, backing West and sniping at Swift via Twitter and Instagram.

## FIGHTING WORDS

But the public bickering paled in light of Kanye West's remarks on *TMZ Live* in May 2018. During his appearance on the show, which airs tabloid news stories on television and the internet, West said, "When you hear about slavery for 400 years—for 400 years? That sounds like a choice." Angry comments flooding social media showed that many believed West was blaming black people for their own enslavement.

The backlash was immediate. Many celebrities publicly criticized West on TV and social media, claiming his words demonstrated an ignorance of history. In the lyrics to one of his raps, "Wouldn't Leave," West revealed how his wife had panicked after the broadcast. She worried that the blowback would have a negative impact on both of their brands.

## KIM'S KONTROVERSIES

Although West has proven himself to be a magnet for controversy, Kardashian West has sparked a few dust-ups of her own. In the aftermath of Ariana Grande's 2017 concert in Manchester, England, in which a suicide bomb attack left twenty-two people dead, Kardashian West posted a picture of herself and sister Kendall Jenner happily partying with the singer. Kardashian West shared the image along with a message declaring, "Concerts are supposed to be a place where u can let loose and have fun." She later deleted the posting after people complained that she had exploited the tragedy to post another pretty picture of herself.

While promoting her new line of "Kimojis," the reality star took flak for creating an emoji of herself as the Virgin Mary. Many fans were especially offended because Kardashian West is a Christian, yet

## KANYE WEST'S MOST OUTRAGEOUS REMARKS

Never one to downplay his own talents, West has made plenty of over-the-top claims about himself, including the following as reported in *Marie Claire UK*:

- "I am the number one human being in music. That means that any person that's living or breathing is number two."
- "I think what Kanye West is going to be is something similar to what Steve Jobs means."
- "I will go down as the voice of this generation, of this decade, I will be the loudest voice."
- "I will be the leader of a company that ends up being worth billions of dollars, because I got the answers. I understand culture. I am the nucleus."

she seemed to be mocking religion. One Instagram follower scolded her: "you and your husband need to stop thinking you guys are gods."

## PLAYING GOD

In 2006, Kanye West posed on the cover of *Rolling Stone* magazine wearing a bloody crown of thorns. It wouldn't be the only time that West seemed to compare himself to Jesus Christ: in 2013, West released an album titled *Yeezus,* which includes the single "I Am a God."

## "I AM THE MOST POWERFUL VOICE IN MEDIA"

Even West's most loyal fans admit he has a big mouth and an even bigger ego. However, between 2017 and 2018 it became clear that something else might account for West's most controversial behavior.

## SUPERPOWER OR DISABILITY?

In 2018, West released his album *Ye*, which proclaims on the cover, "I hate being bipolar. It's awesome." West references the disorder in his lyrics as well. Bipolar disorder causes unusual shifts in mood, energy, and activity levels. There is no single known cause for the disorder, though genetics may play a role.

People with bipolar disorder may experience manic episodes, periods of being extremely up and energized, and depressive episodes, when they feel very down and hopeless. When these episodes become extreme, an individual may experience psychotic symptoms. If the psychosis occurs during a manic episode, the person may believe he or she has special powers or is famous; if it occurs during a depressive episode, the individual may imagine he or she has committed a crime or is penniless.

If West's diagnosis was accurate, the artist's controversial rants on television and radio shows and his grandiose statements might be expressions of a manic episode. Bipolar disorder is a lifelong illness, but it can be controlled with a combination of medication and psychotherapy. Between manic or depressive episodes, a person with the disorder may be free of symptoms.

With the release of *Ye*, West began to speak frankly about being bipolar, which he has called his superpower, the source of his creativity. In 2016, West was hospitalized with exhaustion and had to cancel some scheduled concerts. Despite exhibiting symptoms for years, West wasn't officially diagnosed with bipolar disorder until 2018, when he was thirty-nine. West admitted that some of his most controversial statements happened during manic episodes. However, during a much-publicized meeting with President Donald Trump in October 2018, West implied that he had been misdiagnosed.

## CHAPTER 6

# POLITICAL POWER COUPLE

With fans all around the world, including millions of followers on social media platforms such as Twitter and Instagram who obsess over their every tweet and posting, Kanye West and Kim Kardashian West can amplify issues and causes that they believe deserve more attention.

## HISTORY'S LESSONS

In 2015, Kim and her sister Khloé visited a memorial outside Yerevan, Armenia, dedicated to the 1.5 million victims massacred by Ottoman Turks in an event known as the Armenian genocide. Whether or not

# KIM KARDASHIAN WEST AND KANYE WEST

> Kim (*left*) and sister Khloé (*center*) visited a memorial to the Armenian genocide. The steep steps leading down to the eternal flame force visitors to bow their heads as they descend.

to use the term "genocide" to describe what happened to Armenians expelled from Turkey is a charged political issue. The United States does not officially recognize the event as a genocide, and Kardashian West has been petitioning to change that.

As a person of Armenian heritage, Kardashian West was outraged in 2016 when the *Wall Street Journal* published an ad by a company that denies the genocide and blames what happened on the Armenians themselves. In response, Kardashian West took out a full-page ad in the *New York Times*, entitled "Genocide Denial Cannot Be Allowed." She asked, "If this had been an ad denying the Holocaust, or pushing some 9/11 conspiracy theory, would it have made it to print?" Kardashian West went on to draw a parallel between the Jewish genocide during World War II and what happened to her own ancestors:

## POLITICAL POWER COUPLE

"In 1939, a week before the Nazi invasion of Poland, Hitler said, 'Who, after all, speaks today of the annihilation of the Armenians?' We do. We must. We must talk about it until it is recognized by our government because when we deny our past, we endanger our future."

> We must talk about [the annihilation of the Armenians] until it is recognized by our government because when we deny our past, we endanger our future."
> —KIM KARDASHIAN WEST

## THE ARMENIAN GENOCIDE

During World War I (1914-1918), the Turkish government embarked on a plan to destroy the entire Armenian population of Turkey. As with many conflicts between different groups of people, this one was rooted in religion: the Ottoman Turks were Muslim, whereas the Armenians practiced Christianity. Between 1915 and the early 1920s, Christian Armenians were subject to deportation, abduction, torture, massacre, and starvation. According to the *New York Times*, the Ottoman Turks systematically slaughtered 1.5 million Armenians and other minorities, and many more were forcibly removed from the country. However, the Turkish government has never acknowledged the enormity of these events, and people in Turkey have been jailed for using the term "genocide" to refer to what happened to the Armenians.

## AN UNPOPULAR POSITION

Kanye West's politics do not always sit well with his fans. In the aftermath of the contentious 2016 US presidential election, West dismayed members of the hip-hop community by tweeting positively about Donald Trump, who beat Hillary Clinton in Electoral College votes to become the forty-fifth president of the United States. (Clinton won the US popular vote.) West met with the president-elect in Trump Tower, and the two reportedly discussed issues including supporting teachers, modernizing curricula, and the ongoing violence in Chicago.

Plenty of West's fans didn't approve of him backing a man who disrespected women, as shown by the

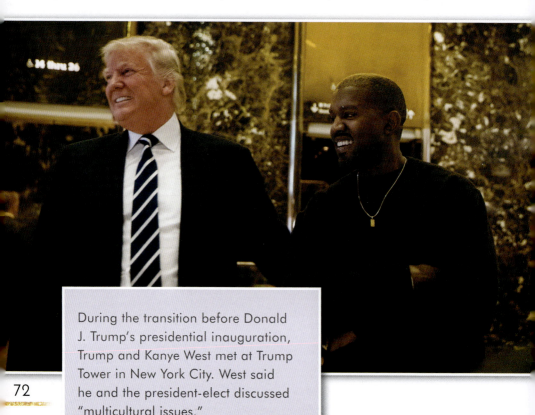

During the transition before Donald J. Trump's presidential inauguration, Trump and Kanye West met at Trump Tower in New York City. West said he and the president-elect discussed "multicultural issues."

vulgar remarks Trump made to the host of *Access Hollywood* and that were captured on tape. They also knew Trump had a history of racist behavior and had pushed the right-wing conspiracy that questioned whether President Barack Obama had an American birth certificate. During a concert in San Jose, California, when West announced that he would have voted for Trump, he got booed.

## DOUBLING DOWN

Then, during the summer of 2017, President Trump failed to outright condemn white supremacists who marched in Charlottesville, Virginia, displaying swastikas and Confederate flags. Trump's insistence that "both sides" were to blame for the fatal rioting that followed troubled many observers. Yet West tweeted that "the mob can't make me not love him. We are both dragon energy. He is my brother." He also posted a picture of himself wearing a red baseball cap emblazoned with the Trump campaign's slogan, Make American Great Again.

## PUSHBACK

West's friends and fellow rappers have called him out for supporting Trump. Singer John Legend, a close friend and frequent collaborator, texted West a heartfelt message, which Kanye shared on Twitter: "So many people who love you feel so betrayed right now because they know the harm that Trump's policies cause, especially to people of color. Don't let this be part of your legacy. You're the greatest artist of our generation." Kardashian West, who had supported Hillary Clinton during the election, urged West to explain that he didn't approve of everything the president was doing. Some people even blamed West's mental health problems for his love of Trump.

## LOBBYING FOR JUSTICE

Kanye West isn't the only member of this power couple who has met with President Trump. In May 2018, Kim Kardashian West visited the White House to discuss prison reform and to lobby for the pardon of an African American woman named Alice Marie Johnson. In 1996, Johnson had been found guilty of participating in a multimillion-dollar cocaine-distribution ring, and she was sentenced to life in prison. Johnson was tried and sentenced in federal court, where there is no possibility of parole.

In the US justice system, people of color often receive longer sentences for their crimes than their white counterparts, according to a 2017 report by the US Sentencing Commission. Kardashian West heard about Johnson's case and began tweeting about it. She felt it was unfair that Johnson, now a sixty-three-year-old grandmother, had been incarcerated for decades for a first-time, nonviolent offense.

US presidents have the power to grant pardons to people convicted of federal crimes. When Kardashian

POLITICAL POWER COUPLE

In May 2018, Kim Kardashian West met with President Trump in the Oval Office at the White House. The two met again in September 2018 to continue their discussion about prison reform.

West met with President Trump in the Oval Office, he agreed to commute Johnson's life sentence. She called Johnson in person to give her the news that she would be freed after twenty-one years of incarceration. Kardashian West tweeted that she hopes to continue working for prison reform "with organizations who have been fighting this fight for much longer than I have and deserve the recognition."

75

## MONOPOLIZING THE CONVERSATION

On October 11, 2018, Kanye West again met with President Trump, this time in the Oval Office, along with retired football player Jim Brown. Surrounded by photographers, the three men discussed a range of topics—or West talked and Trump and Brown mostly

## #ENOUGH

On Valentine's Day 2018, a gunman opened fire at Marjorie Stoneman Douglas High School in Parkland, Florida, killing seventeen students and staff members and injuring many others. The shooter, a former student of the school, was apprehended after the shootings.

According to CNN, the United States has fifty-seven times as many school shootings as all other industrialized nations combined, yet efforts to pass new gun legislation in the wake of these recurring tragedies have repeatedly failed. Students at the high school who survived the shooting wanted this time to be different. They poured their grief and anger into political activism, tweeting the hashtag #ENOUGH and organizing the March for Our Lives. This massive protest took place just thirty-eight days after the shooting and inspired similar marches throughout the United States and across the world. Parkland student activists such as Emma González and David Hogg have become powerful voices in the national debate about gun violence.

listened. West's rambling monologue—which touched on everything from his own wealth and IQ, the Thirteenth Amendment to the Constitution, and hydrogen-powered planes—left many observers scratching their heads.

## MARCHING AGAINST GUN VIOLENCE

The star power that celebrities wield can help shine a spotlight on the causes they believe in. Both Kardashian West and West have spoken out against gun violence in the United States. Even before she was robbed at gunpoint in Paris, Kim had been working with Everytown for Gun Safety, an organization pushing for common-sense legislation on firearms.

On March 24, 2018, the husband-and-wife team attended the March for Our Lives with their four-year-old daughter, North. Organized by the student survivors of the Parkland school massacre, the Washington, DC, event drew a crowd of more than two million people demanding government action on gun reform.

## YE FOR PRESIDENT?

After the 2016 presidential election, many people with no experience in politics began to feel like they might have a shot at the US presidency. After all, if a businessman and reality TV star like Donald Trump could get elected, why not them? Not surprisingly,

Kanye West has his own political ambitions. "Rappers are the philosophers of now, celebrities are the influencers of our now, just look at the president," West told fans during a 2016 concert in San Jose, California. At the 2016 MTV Video Music Awards, he announced, "I have decided, in 2020, to run for president." He later adjusted his timeline, tweeting the hashtag #Kanye2024.

West appeared to be serious about becoming a candidate. He told *Vanity Fair*, "I didn't approach that because I thought it would be fun ... No, the exact opposite. I sit in clubs and I'm like, Wow, I've got five years before I go and run for office and I've got a lot of research to do, I've got a lot of growing up to do." West joked that he isn't a Republican or a Democrat but would form his own party—called the Birthday Party.

# CHAPTER 7

# PLANS FOR WORLD DOMINATION

By the end of 2018, Kanye West and Kim Kardashian West had accumulated power, wealth, and influence beyond the average person's wildest dreams. They also had three beautiful children to keep them busy. They had donated their time and money to causes they believed in, received a warm welcome at the White House, and West had announced his plan to run for the top office in the land.

So, what would be the couple's next move? When you've already accomplished all of your goals, what on earth do you do next?

## BOUNDLESS AMBITIONS

Need proof that Kanye West is playing the long game? Back in 2012, he created an imaginary organizational chart for a business called the Donda Communications Company. The chart shows tentacles reaching into multiple "categories of influence," including lifestyle, health and wellness, transportation, finance, and alternative energy sources. One day soon, you may be wearing the latest style of Yeezy sneakers while sitting on your Ye-designed couch using your Ye mobile phone while you pay for a ticket on Ye airlines with your Ye credit card.

## KIM'S BUSINESS EMPIRE

Kim Kardashian West has one of the most recognizable brands on the planet. By 2018, the reality TV star and second-richest member of the Kardashian clan (sister Kendell Jenner was richer) could add the titles of executive producer, businesswoman, entrepreneur, and mobile mogul to her impressive résumé.

### MOBILE MOGUL

In 2014, Kardashian West launched a massively successful online role-playing game called *Kim Kardashian: Hollywood*. Players create their own aspiring celebrity, befriend Kim, and work their way from the E-list up to the A-list by boosting their fame and reputation. They can even become part of a virtual

# PLANS FOR WORLD DOMINATION

power couple. Initially, players download the games for free; later they can purchase extras through the app.

A year later, Kardashian West launched her mobile app Kimoji, which gives users access to custom Kim-related emojis, virtual stickers, and GIFs. According to TMZ, when Kimoji was launched more than nine thousand downloads occurred per milli-second. On December 21, 2015, Kardashian West tweeted "Apple, so sorry I broke your App Store!!!" Another app awards

Some of the settings and events featured in *Kim Kardashian: Hollywood* are based on actual events in Kim's life and places she and her family have visited.

Apple, so sorry I broke your App Store!!!"
—KIM KARDASHIAN WEST

81

paying users with access to beauty tutorials and exclusive Kardashian content. In December 2018, Kardashian West announced that she would be shutting down her subscription-based personal apps in 2019. Other apps, including the Kimoji app, would continue to operate, according to Kris Holt of Engadget.com.

## BEAUTY BONANZA

Kanye West once remarked on a Los Angeles radio show that his wife is "talented at being beautiful," and Kardashian West has monetized her looks into a booming business. In June 2017, she launched her own makeup line, KKW Beauty. Within hours of the launch, all products had sold out, bringing in an estimated $14.4 million, according to Rachel Strugatz on WWD.com.

Not surprisingly, Kanye West has his own plans for the makeup market. In 2017, he filed paperwork to start his own beauty brand called Donda Cosmetics. The company will produce makeup, lotions, and fragrances.

## THE SWEET SMELL OF SUCCESS

Kardashian West began selling perfume in 2009, starting with her signature scent, Kim Kardashian. Since then, she has added six additional perfumes to the Kim Kardashian Fragrance line. In 2018, she announced a scented spin-off of her Kimoji app: KKW Kimoji Fragrance perfume.

Kim and Kanye are pictured here with Saint (*left*) and North (*right*) in New York City in 2016. Their third child, Chi, was born in 2018.

## BEST-DRESSED BABIES

In 2017, the power parents embarked on a joint venture inspired by their mutual love of fashion: Kids Supply. The online brand of stylish children's apparel sells customizable Yeezy sneakers, mini satin bomber jackets, and other garments. West and Kardashian West have included their kids in the production process—North and Saint offer their opinions about sample fabrics and wear-test the clothes themselves.

Following in her parents' fashionable footsteps, five-year-old North West had her runway debut in the fall of 2018 as a model at an L.O.L. Surprise fashion show in Los Angeles.

## COLLABORATIONS AND CONFLICT

Kanye West may be running for president and drawing up his plans to take over the world, but he still finds time to make music, usually in collaboration with other musicians. In June 2018, he staged a "listening party" in Jackson Hole, Wyoming, to celebrate the release of his *Ye* album. The scenic setting became a creative sanctuary for West after he was hospitalized in 2016 for exhaustion. In 2018, he teamed up with rap artist and actor Kid Cudi to produce *Kids See Ghosts*. West also announced the upcoming release of his thirteenth album, titled *Yandhi*, but at the beginning of 2019 that project was still on hold.

PLANS FOR WORLD DOMINATION

The power couple meet with children at an orphanage in Uganda in October 2018. West traveled to the East African nation to finish work on his album *Yandhi*.

In true Ye fashion, he has continued to act as a lightning rod for controversy, behaving erratically on *Saturday Night Live* and engaging in public feuds with the rap star Drake and even with his own mother-in-law, Kris Jenner.

## AN ARTIST"S LEGACY

In his 2015 interview for the *Time* 100 issue, Kanye West declared, "I don't care about having a legacy. I don't care about being remembered." Whether or not he thinks much about what he will leave behind, West has already had an indelible impact on American music. His songs have repeatedly challenged the rules of hip-hop, enlarging its subject matter and enriching its emotional terrain. West opened up possibilities for social awareness in rap music and called out its homophobia. Successful rap artists such as Travis Scott, Chance the Rapper, J. Cole, and Drake all owe a debt to Ye.

## A KANYE WEST DISCOGRAPHY

The following is a chronological list of Kanye West's albums (as of January 2019):

*The College Dropout* (2004)
*Late Registration* (2005)
*Late Orchestration: Live at Abbey Road Studios* (2006)
*Graduation* (2007)
*808s & Heartbreak* (2008)
*My Beautiful Dark Twisted Fantasy* (2010)
*Watch the Throne* (2011)
*Yeezus* (2013)
*The Life of Pablo* (2016)
*Ye* (2018)
*Kids See Ghosts* (2018)
*Yandhi* (Release date delayed)

## MAKING THE MOST OF IT

In the course of their careers, Kanye West and Kim Kardashian West have proved wrong many people who once doubted their abilities. Initially dismissed by those who saw her as an attractive socialite with no talent, Kardashian West went on to become a highly respected businesswoman and multimillionaire.

Rappers once looked at Kanye West in his polo shirts and assumed he'd never make it in their world, yet today he is considered one of the most talented rap musicians on record, not to mention a successful fashion designer and multifaceted entrepreneur with big plans for the future.

Through a combination of talent, luck, controversy, and hard work, they have become two of the best-known humans on Earth. At the end of 2018, the two continued to set social media on fire with antics such as flying to Tokyo, Japan, in an otherwise empty 747, and presenting the Ugandan despot President Yoweri Museveni with a pair of signed Yeezy sneakers during a trip to Africa. Clearly, Kanye and Kim aren't planning to give up their place in the world's spotlight anytime soon. If you're ever in London, you can visit Madame Tussauds legendary museum and snap a selfie with the wax sculptures of this acclaimed power couple, looking their very best, posing for posterity.

# TIMELINE

**1977** Kanye West is born on June 8 in Atlanta, Georgia.

**1980** Kimberly Noel Kardashian is born on October 21 in Los Angeles, California.

**2002** Kanye West is involved in a serious car accident in Los Angeles on October 23.

**2003** Robert Kardashian dies of esophageal cancer on September 30.

**2006** On February 8, Kanye West becomes the first solo artist to have his first three studio albums nominated for Album of the Year at the Grammy Awards.

**2007** The first season of *Keeping Up with the Kardashians* airs on October 14 on the E! network. On November 10, Donda West dies after undergoing cosmetic surgery.

**2013** Kanye West and Kim Kardashian's first child, North West, is born on June 15. On October 21, West proposes to Kardashian in San Francisco, California.

**2014** Kardashian and West are married on May 24 in Florence, Italy.

**2015** Kanye West receives an honorary PhD in his hometown of Chicago. Kardashian West and West appear in the *Time* 100 issue of the World's Most Influential People. On

# TIMELINE

December 5, the couple's second child, Saint West, is born.

**2016** Kardashian West is tied up and robbed at gunpoint in her Paris hotel.

**2017** Kanye West ties Jay-Z for most Grammy wins by a rap artist (twenty-one).

**2018** The couple's second daughter, Chicago (Chi) West, is born via surrogate on January 15. Kim Kardashian West successfully lobbies President Donald Trump to pardon Alice Marie Johnson on June 6. On October 11, Kanye West meets with Trump in the Oval Office.

**2019** In January, Kardashian West and West confirmed that they were expecting their fourth child, a boy, to be born by surrogate.

# GLOSSARY

**beat** A hip-hop instrumental. A typical hip-hop song consists of a beat and vocals.

**bipolar disorder** A mental disorder marked by alternating periods of mania and depression.

**born-again** Experienced a spiritual rebirth. A born-again Christian is a person who has converted to a personal faith in Jesus Christ.

**break the internet** To cause a commotion that has many social networking sites and news outlets all discussing the same thing.

**despot** A tyrannical ruler with absolute power and authority.

**emoji** A small digital image or icon used to express an emotion or idea in digital communication.

**esophageal cancer** Cancer that occurs in the esophagus, the long hollow tube that delivers food from the mouth to the stomach.

**genocide** The deliberate killing of a large group of people, especially those of a particular ethnic group or nation.

**hip-hop** A cultural movement that attained widespread popularity in the 1980s and 1990s; also the backing music for rap.

**mogul** An important or powerful person, most often in the motion picture or media industry.

**narcissistic** Having an obsessive interest in oneself or in one's appearance.

**not safe (or suitable) for work (NSFW)** The term indicates an image or text that contains potentially inappropriate content.

# GLOSSARY

**paparazzi** Freelance photographers who take pictures of celebrities.

**platinum record** Awarded to a singer or group whose album has sold one million copies.

**pop** A genre of popular music that originated in the United States and the United Kingdom in the mid-1950s. Pop can include many different styles of music.

**rap** A musical style in which rhythmic or rhyming speech is chanted to musical accompaniment; (verb) To recite words in rhythm over music.

**reality TV** Television programs in which real people are continuously filmed. Unlike documentaries, reality shows are meant to be entertaining rather than informative.

**royalties** Payments to an owner for the ongoing use of their asset or property. In the music industry, songwriters receive royalties when their music is used on CDs, records, and tapes. The royalty payment is based on sales.

**samples** Short portions of previously recorded music that are used in a new song.

**socialite** A person well known in fashionable society who enjoys social activities.

**soul** A kind of music incorporating elements of rhythm and blues (R&B) and gospel music, popularized by African Americans.

**surrogate** A traditional surrogate is a woman whose own egg is artificially inseminated with a father's sperm. A gestational surrogate has a fertilized embryo implanted in her uterus and carries the fetus until birth.

**synesthesia** A neurological condition that causes the brain to process data in the form of several senses at once. A synesthete may hear sounds while also seeing them as colorful swirls.

**telegenic** Having an appearance and manner that are attractive to television viewers.

**turntable** The circular, revolving plate used to support a record as it is played.

# FOR MORE INFORMATION

AllMusic.com
Website: https://allmusic.com/artist/kanye
   -west-mn0000361014/biography
Facebook: @AllMusicDotCom
Twitter: @allmusic
This music website includes a Kanye West
   biography, along with a discography, album
   highlights, list of songs, production credits,
   and awards.

Bata Shoe Museum
327 Bloor Street West
Toronto, ON M5S 1W7
Canada
(416) 979-7799
Website: http://batashoemuseum.ca
Facebook and Twitter: @batashoemuseum
The museum houses four galleries celebrating
   the style and function of footwear,
   ranging from ancient Egyptian sandals to
   contemporary shoe styles.

Billboard.com
Website: https://billboard.com/hip-hop-rap-r-and-b
Facebook: @Billboard
Twitter: @billboard
This online extension of *Billboard* magazine offers
   music industry news, videos, podcasts, photos,
   and Billboard charts with samples for R&B/hip-
   hop, pop, Latin, and other genres of music.

Grammy Museum
800 West Olympic Boulevard
Los Angeles, CA 90015
(213) 765-6800
Website: https://grammymuseum.org
Facebook: @grammymuseum
Twitter: @GRAMMYmuseum
Opened in 2008, the Grammy Museum uses interactive exhibits to explore and celebrate the art and technology of the recording process and the legacy of all forms of recorded music.

Hip-Hop: Beyond Beats and Rhymes
Website: http://www.pbs.org/independentlens/hiphop/index.htm
This online companion to the film examines the underlying issues in hip-hop culture, including violence, misogyny, and homophobia. The website includes a timeline of hip-hop history and a glossary of key terms.

Hip-Hop Canada
Website: https://hiphopcanada.com
Facebook: @hiphopcanadacom
Twitter: @HipHopCanada
This is a comprehensive website devoted to the Canadian hip-hop scene featuring news, music reviews, podcasts, music videos, and event and music festival lists.

## FOR MORE INFORMATION

Madame Tussauds Hollywood
6933 Hollywood Boulevard
Hollywood, CA 90038
(323) 798-1670
Website: https://www.madametussauds.com
   /hollywood
Facebook: @MadameTussaudsHollywood
Twitter: @TussaudsLA
Founded by wax sculptor Madame "Marie" Tussauds in 1761, this famous wax museum now has branches all over the world. The museum displays lifelike wax sculptures of celebrities, movie characters, and famous figures from history. The Hollywood Branch of Madame Tussauds features wax statues of Kim Kardashian West and other members of the Kardashian-Jenner clan.

Museum of the Moving Image
36-01 36th Avenue
Astoria, NY 11106
(718) 777-6888
Website: http://www.movingimage.us
Facebook: @MovingImageMuseum
Twitter: @MovingImageNYC
The only museum in the United States devoted to the art, history, technique, and technology of the moving image in all its forms. In addition to its core collection, the museum offers changing exhibitions, discussions with

leading figures in the film and television industries, and online projects.

Ranker
6420 Wilshire Boulevard, Suite 500
Los Angeles, CA 90048
Website: https://www.ranker.com/list/best-canadian-rappers/ranker-hip-hop
Facebook: @Ranker
Ranker offers crowdsourced polls across a range of topics, including music and entertainment. Find out how visitors ranked Canadian rappers and vote for your own favorites.

Reality Blurred
Website: https://realityblurred.com
This guide to the world of reality television contains news, reviews, and analysis, as well as TV schedules, behind-the-scene reports, and interviews with reality TV cast members and producers.

Beaumont, Mark. *Kanye West: God & Monster*. London, UK: Overlook Omnibus, 2015.

Halperin, Ian. *Kardashian Dynasty*. New York, NY: Gallery Books, 2016.

Oppenheimer, Jerry. *The Kardashians: An American Drama*. New York, NY: St. Martin's Press, 2017.

Ouellette, Laurie. *A Companion to Reality Television*. Chichester, UK: Wiley Blackwell, 2017.

Sacks, Nathan. *American Hip-Hop: Rappers, DJs, and Hard Beats*. Minneapolis, MN: Twenty-First Century Books, 2013.

Saddleback Educational Publishing. *Jay-Z (Hip-Hop Biographies)*. Costa Mesa, CA: Saddleback Publishing, 2013.

Saddleback Educational Publishing. *Kanye West (Hip-Hop Biographies)*. Costa Mesa, CA: Saddleback Publishing, 2013.

Smith, Sean. *Kim*. New York, NY: HarperCollins, 2015.

Thompson, Tamara. *Rap and Hip-Hop*. Detroit, MI: Greenhaven Publishing, 2013.

Toobin, Jeffrey. *The Run of His Life: The People vs. O. J. Simpson*. New York, NY: Random House, 2015.

Walrath, Dana. *Like Water on Stone*. New York, NY: Delacorte Press, 2014.

West, Donda. *Raising Kanye: Life Lessons from the Mother of a Hip-Hop Superstar*. New York, NY: Pocket Books, 2007.

# BIBLIOGRAPHY

A&E Television Network. "Kanye West." Biography.com, June 13, 2018. https://www.biography.com/people/kanye-west-362922.

Baker, Soren. *The History of Rap and Hip-Hop.* Farmington Hills, MI: Lucent Books, 2012.

Barker, Emily. "Every Preposterous Comparison Kanye West Has Made Between Himself and These Cultural Icons." *NME*, October 2, 2015. https://www.nme.com/photos/every-preposterous-comparison-kanye-west-has-made-between-himself-and-these-cultural-icons-1421468.

Baron, Zach. "Kanye West: A Brand-New Ye." *GQ*, July 20, 2014. https://www.gq.com/story/kanye-west.

Barsamian, Edward. "Kim and Kanye Are Here with More Kids' Clothes." *Vogue*, September 15, 2017. https://www.vogue.com/article/kanye-west-kim-kardashian-west-north-west-saint-west-the-kids-supply-celebrity-family-style.

BBC News. "Kim and Kanye Meeting Ugandan President Yoweri Museveni Was Controversial." BBC.com, October 16, 2018. https://www.bbc.com/news/newsbeat-45834730.

Beaumont, Mark. *Kanye West: God & Monster.* New York, NY: Omnibus Press, 2015.

Borrelli, Christopher. "'College Dropout' to PhD: Kanye West Receives Honorary Doctorate in Chicago." *Chicago Tribune,* May 15, 2015. http://www.chicagotribune.com/entertainment

/music/ct-kanye-west-saic-commencement-20150511-story.html.

Bush, George. Interview with Matt Lauer. *Today*, November 5, 2010. https://www.youtube.com/watch?v=lYrU-Exhklo.

Caramanica, Jon. "The Agony and the Ecstasy of Kanye West." *New York Times*, April 10, 2015. https://www.nytimes.com/2015/04/10/t-magazine/kanye-west-adidas-yeezy-fashion-interview.html.

Chapin, Adele. "The 10 Most Kanye Quotes from Kanye West's Style.com Interview." Racked.com, February 16, 2015. https://www.racked.com/2015/2/16/8047469/kanye-west-adidas-fashion-week-quotes.

Charity, Justin. "The Kim Kardashian Guide to American Politics." Theringer.com, June 7, 2018. https://www.theringer.com/2018/6/7/17436558/kim-kardashian-alice-marie-johnson-donald-trump.

CNN Library. Hurricane Katrina Statistics Fast Facts. CNN, August 30, 2018. https://www.cnn.com/2013/08/23/us/hurricane-katrina-statistics-fast-facts/index.html.

Complex. "R.I.P. Pastelle: A History of Kanye West's Lost Clothing Line." *Complex*, October 14, 2009. https://www.complex.com/style/2009/10/r-i-p-pastelle-a-history-of-kanyes-lost-clothing-line.

Cronin, Travis, and Esther Lee. "Tim Gunn Flips Through Kim Kardashian's Selfie Book *Selfish*."

*US*, June 5, 2015. https://www.usmagazine.com/celebrity-news/news/tim-gunn-flips-through-kim-kardashian-selfie-book-iq-is-plummeting-201556/.

Edwards, Paul. *The Concise Guide to Hip-Hop Music.* New York, NY: St. Martin's Griffin, 2015.

Gavilanes, Grace. "Inside Kanye West and Jay-Z's Tumultuous Relationship through the Years." *People*, May 2, 2018. https://people.com/music/kanye-west-jay-z-friendship-timeline.

Grabow, Chip, and Lisa Rose. "The US Has Had 57 as Many School Shootings as the Other Major Industrialized Nations Combined." CNN, May 21, 2018. https://www.cnn.com/2018/05/21/us/school-shooting-us-versus-world-trnd/index.html.

Gray, Mark. "Kim Kardashian Recalls Her Birthday at Neverland." *People*, June 27, 2009. https://people.com/celebrity/kim-kardashian-recalls-her-birthday-at-neverland.

Green, Matt. *The Amazing Life of Kanye West* (Celebrity Biographies). Google Play Edition (Ebook), 2017.

History.com. "The Armenian Genocide." October 1, 2010. https://www.history.com/topics/world-war-i/armenian-genocide.

Holt, Kris. "Kardashian-Jenner Sisters Will Close Their Subscription Apps in 2018." Engadget.com, December 20, 2018. https://www.engadget.com/2018/12/20/kardashian

-jenner-subscription-apps-shutting-down.
Huffington Post. "Kim Kardashian's Ex Damon Thomas." Updated December 6, 2017. https://www.huffingtonpost.com/2010/05/05/kim-kardashians-ex-damon_n_563949.html.
Imbd.com. "Kim Kardashian West: Biography." Retrieved September 20, 2018. https://www.imdb.com/name/nm2578007/bio.
Kardashian, Kim. *Kourtney and Kim Take New York*. Season 1, episode one, January 2011.
Kardashian, Kim. Interview with Ryan Seacrest. February 25, 2014. KIIS FM Radio.
Kardashian, Khloé, Kourtney Kardashian, and Kim Kardashian. *Kardashian Konfidential*. New York, NY: St. Martin's Press, 2010.
Kifner, John. "Armenian Genocide of 1915: An Overview." *New York Times*. Retrieved November 1, 2018. https://archive.nytimes.com/www.nytimes.com/ref/timestopics/topics_armeniangenocide.html?mcubz.
Legend, John (@johnlegend). "So many people who love you feel so betrayed right now because they know the harm that Trump's policies cause, especially to people of color. Don't let this be part of your legacy. You're the greatest artist of our generation," Twitter text, retweeted by @KanyeWest April 26, 2018.
Lupica, Lilith Hardie. "Kim Kardashian West's Surrogate Speaks Out About Carrying Chicago West for the First Time." *Vogue*, March 8, 2018.

https://www.vogue.com.au/celebrity/news/kim-kardashian-wests-surrogate-speaks-out-about-carrying-chicago-west-for-the-first-time/news-story/41b597d423b87febc744c830ba4b7c93.

Mandell, Andrea. "Anna Wintour: Kanye Did Not Beg for Cover." *USA Today*, March 21, 2014. https://www.usatoday.com/story/life/people/2014/03/21/anna-wintour-comments-on-rumors-kanye-west-begged-for-cover/6700983.

Mattern, Joanne. *Kim Kardashian: Reality TV Star.* North Mankato, MN: ABDO Publishing, 2012.

Morgan, Kayla. *Kanye West: Soul-Fired Hip-Hop.* Minneapolis, MN: Twenty-First Century Books, 2013.

MTV. Interview with Kanye West, 2002. Published January 12, 2018. https://www.youtube.com/watch?v=AwbSTjCRQDQ.

MTV. Video Music Awards. September 13, 2009. https://www.youtube.com/watch?v=1z8gCZ7zpsQ.

National Institute of Mental Health. "Bipolar Disorder." NIMH.NIH.gov, April 2016. https://www.nimh.nih.gov/health/topics/bipolar-disorder/index.shtml.

NBC. "A Concert for Hurricane Relief." Broadcast September 2, 2005.

*New York Times.* "Celebrities Books, Best Sellers." June 14, 2015. https://www.nytimes.com

/books/best-sellers/2015/06/14/celebrities.

Oppenheimer, Jerry. *The Kardashians: An American Drama*. New York, NY: St. Martin's Press, 2017.

Page, Vanessa. "Kim Kardashian: Net Worth." Investopedia.com. Retrieved November 2, 2018. https://www.investopedia.com/university/kim-kardashian-biography/kim-kardashian-net-worth.asp.

Ramsdale, Suzannah. "'I Am God's Vessel': Kanye West's Most WTF Quotes." *Marie Claire UK*, November 18, 2016. https://www.marieclaire.co.uk/entertainment/people/the-best-kanye-west-quotes-80943.

Robehmed, Natalie. "Top-Earning Reality Stars 2016." *Forbes*, November 16, 2016. https://www.forbes.com/sites/natalierobehmed/2016/11/16/top-earning-reality-stars-2016-kardashians-jenners-combine-for-122-5-million/#23dd21f4274d.

*Rolling Stone*. "Album Reviews." November 25, 2010. https://www.rollingstone.com/music/music-album-reviews/my-beautiful-dark-twisted-fantasy-120679.

*Rolling Stone*. "Kimye: A Love Story Timeline." July 8, 2015. https://www.rollingstone.com/music/music-news/kimye-a-love-story-timeline-57335.

Ross, Janell. "Two Decades Later, Black and White Americans Finally Agree on O. J. Simpson's Guilt." *Washington Post*, March 4, 2016.

https://www.washingtonpost.com/news/the-fix/wp/2015/09/25/black-and-white-americans-can-now-agree-o-j-was-guilty/?noredirect=on&utm_term=.84ef86ad86cb.

Sacks, Nathan. *American Hip-Hop: Rappers, DJs, and Hard Beats*. Minneapolis, MN: Twenty-First Century Books, 2013.

Saddleback Educational Publishing. *Kanye West* (Hip-Hop Biographies). Costa Mesa, CA: Saddleback Publishing, 2013.

Schmidt, Mackenzie. "Kim Kardashian and Kanye West Called 'Obnoxious,' 'Wasteful," for Flying on Private, Empty 747. *People*, November 27, 2018. https://people.com/home/kim-kardashian-and-kanye-west-called-obnoxious-wasteful-for-flying-on-private-empty-747.

Schreffler, Laura. "Man of Distinction: Ryan Seacrest Strives for Greatness Every Day." Hauteliving.com, January 15, 2015. http://hauteliving.com/2015/01/man-distinction-ryan-seacrest-strives-greatness-every-day/541680.

Seal, Mark. "The Inside Story of the Kim Kardashian Paris Hotel Heist." *Vanity Fair*, November 22, 2016. https://www.vanityfair.com/style/2016/10/solving-kim-kardashian-west-paris-robbery.

Strachan, Maxwell. "The Definitive History of 'George Bush Doesn't Care about Black

People.'" Huffington Post, August 28, 2015. https://www.huffingtonpost.com/entry/kanye-west-george-bush-black-people_us_55d67c12e4b020c386de2f5e.

Strugatz, Rachel. "Kim Kardashian's Makeup Line Expected to Net $14.4 million in Minutes." WWD.com, June 19, 2017. https://wwd.com/beauty-industry-news/color-cosmetics/kim-kardashian-kkw-makeup-interview-business-projections-10917558.

Thomasos, Christine. "Kanye West: Kim Kardashian's Beauty Is Her Talent." Christianpost.com, October 29, 2013. https://www.christianpost.com/news/kanye-west-kim-kardashians-beauty-is-her-talent-107648.

Tikkanen, Amy. "Kim Kardashian: American Television Personality and Entrepreneur." Britannica.com. Retrieved September 20, 2018. https://www.britannica.com/biography/Kim-Kardashian.

*Time.* "The 100 Most Influential People (2015)." Time.com. Retrieved November 3, 2018. http://time.com/collection/2015-time-100.

TMZ Live. Interview with Kanye West. TMZ.com, May 2, 2018. http://www.tmz.com/2018/05/02/tmz-live-kanye.

TMZ Live. "Kim and Kanye 3rd Baby Due in January." TMZ.com, September 6, 2017. https://www.tmz.com/2017/09/06/kim-kardashian-kanye-west-3rd-baby-due.

TMZ Live. "Kim Kardashian: My Kimoji App Messed Up Apple." TMZ.com, December 21, 2015. https://www.tmz.com/2015/12/21/kim-kardashian-kimoji-apple-crash/?vtest=100.

United States Sentencing Commission. "Demographic Differences in Sentencing." November 14, 2017. https://www.ussc.gov/research/research-reports/demographic-differences-sentencing.

*Washington Post*. Transcript of Kanye West's Oval Office Monologue. October 11, 2018. https://www.washingtonpost.com/arts-entertainment/2018/10/11/read-entirety-kanye-wests-uninterrupted-oval-office-monologue-annotated/?utm_term=.44015890af8b.

Weiss, Jeff. "Kanye West Mentor No I.D. Reflects on the Rapper's Hammer Pants-Wearing Days." *Billboard,* October 29, 2015. https://www.billboard.com/articles/columns/the-juice/6745313/kanye-mentor-no-id-on-early-days-mc-hammer-pants.

West, Donda. *Raising Kanye: Life Lessons from the Mother of a Hip-Hop Superstar.* New York, NY: Pocket Books, 2007.

West, Kanye (@KanyeWest). "You don't have to agree with trump but the mob can't make me not love him. We are both dragon energy. He is my brother. I love everyone. I don't agree with everything anyone does. That's what makes us individuals. And we have the right to independent thought." Twitter photo and text,

# BIBLIOGRAPHY

April 25, 2018, 10:30 a.m. https://twitter.com/kanyewest/status/989179757651574784.

West, Kim Kardashian. Ad about the Armenian Genocide. *New York Times,* September 17, 2016.

West, Kim Kardashian (@KimKardashian). "Apple, I'm so sorry I broke your App Store!!!" Twitter text, December 21, 2015, 1:53 p.m. https://twitter.com/kimkardashian/status/679057097074413568?lang=en.

West, Kim Kardashian (@KimKardashian). "Concerts are supposed to be a place where u can let loose & have fun. So scary to not feel safe in this world. @arianagrande I love you." Instagram photo and text, May 23, 2017.

West, Kim Kardashian (@KimKardashian). "I hope to continue this important work by working together with organizations who have been fighting this fight for much longer than I have and deserve the recognition." Twitter text, June 6, 2018, 12:18 p.m. https://twitter.com/KimKardashian/status/1004412177376333829.

Woolf, Jake. "The Unabridged History of Kanye West as Fashion Designer." *GQ,* February 11, 2016. https://www.gq.com/gallery/the=-unabridged-history-of-kanye-west-as-fashion-designer-and-the-11-year-road-to-todays-adidas-show.

Yahoo! Finance. "Kanye West Net Worth." Yahoo! Finance, January 13, 2018. https://finance.yahoo.com/news/kanye-west-net-worth-rapper-100214748.html.

# INDEX

## A
albums, 86
  *College Dropout, The*, 14, 22
  *808s & Heartbreak*, 23
  *Late Registration*, 23
  *My Beautiful Dark Twisted Fantasy*, 24
  *Watch the Throne*, 18
  *Yandhi*, 84
  *Ye*, 67, 84
  *Yeezus*, 67
American Music Awards, 22
Armenian heritage, of Kardashians, 6, 8, 27–28, 44, 69–70, 71

## B
beats, 14, 16–17, 18
BET Visionary Award, 54
Beyoncé, 18, 22, 47, 63–64
bipolar disorder, 67, 68
Bocelli, Andrea, 6, 45
break the internet, incidents of, 49
Bush, George, 63

## C
Christianity
  of Armenians, 71
  of Kim, 66–67
  of Kim and Kanye, 39
  of Robert Kardashian, 29

## D
Dash, Damon, 19, 52, 54
Dupri, Jermaine, 18–19

## E
engagement, of Kim and Kanye, 44

## F
fashion
  hip-hop, 52
  Kanye's interest in, 20, 42–43, 50, 84, 85, 87
  Kim's interest in, 40–41, 84
footwear, designed by Kanye, 50–51

## G
genocide, Armenian, 69–71
Grammys, 22, 23, 52

## H
Hilton, Paris, 27
hip-hop

# INDEX

in Chicago, 16
and fashion, 52
history of, 15–16
Kanye's place in, 8, 10, 12, 23, 72, 86
Kim's connections to, 42
producers in, 16
Humphries, Kris, 35, 42, 43–44
Hurricane Katrina, 61, 62

## I

Instagram, 6, 48, 60, 64–65, 67, 69

## J

Jackson, T. J., 34
Jay-Z, 18, 19, 47, 52
Jenner, Bruce (Caitlyn), 29, 31, 45
Jenner, Kendall, 29, 65–66
Jenner, Kylie, 29
Jenner-Kardashian household, 37, 38, 40, 47, 60
Johnson, Alice Marie, 74–75

## K

Kardashian, Khloé, 26, 36, 45, 69
Kardashian, Kourtney, 26, 35, 36, 45
Kardashian (Jenner), Kris, 25–26, 29, 31, 33, 85
Kardashian, Robert
  Christianity, 29
  death from esophageal cancer, 35
  divorce, 31
  family business, 27–28
  love of Andrea Bocelli, 45
  marriage and family, 25–26
  prophecy of fame, 35
  relationship with children, 34–35
  relationship with O. J. Simpson, 32, 33
*Kardashian Konfidential*, 31, 34, 35, 37
*Keeping Up with the Kardashians* (KUWTK), 38, 42, 43, 51, 60
Kids Supply, 84
*Kim Kardashian: Hollywood*, 80
Kimojis, 66, 81, 82

## L

legacy
 of Kanye, 74, 85–86
 of Robert Kardashian, 34–35
Legend, John, 22, 37, 47, 73–74

## M

makeup, Kim's line, 80
March for Our Lives, 76, 77
Marjorie Stoneman Douglas High School, 76
moguls
 fashion, 52
 Kim as business, 6, 8, 80
 mobile, 80–82
Museveni, Youweri, 87

## N

net worth,
 Kanye's, 51
 of Kardashian-Jenners, 38

## P

paparazzi, 60
platinum record, 22
politics
 American, 77
 of Kanye, 72, 77–78
 of Kim, 69–70
 of Kim and Kanye, 76
 of Ray West, 13

## R

Ramos, Daniel, 60–61
reality TV
 Donald Trump as star, 77
 Kim as star, 6, 8, 37, 80
robbery, of Kim, 60
Roc-A-Fella, 18, 19–20, 52, 54
*Rolling Stone* magazine, 8, 23, 24, 67
RUN DMC, 14, 52

## S

samples, 16
Seacrest, Ryan, 37, 38, 46
security, of West family, 59, 60
*Selfish*, 56
Simpson, O. J., 32
slavery, Kanye's comments on, 65
social media
 criticism on, 65
 followers on, 69

# INDEX

Kim and Kanye on, 8, 87
Kim's break from, 60
Kim's skill at, 27
West children on, 58
Soles4Souls, 53
suicide bomb, attack on Ariana Grande concert, 65
surrogate, birth by, 57, 58
Swift, Taylor, 63–65
synesthesia, 12–13

# T

*Time* 100, 54, 55, 85
Trump, Donald J., 8–9, 68, 72–74, 75, 76–77
Twitter, 64–65, 69, 73–74

# V

Video Music Awards (VMAs), 63–64, 78

# W

weddings
 of Kim and Humphries, 35
 of Kim and Kanye, 6, 18, 44, 45, 46, 47, 48

West, Chicago "Chi," 58
West, Donda, 10, 12, 13, 14, 18, 23, 55
West, North, 43–44, 52–53, 57–58, 77, 84
West, Ray, 10, 12, 13
West, Saint, 57, 84
 delivery of, 58

## ABOUT THE AUTHOR

Monique Vescia has written scores of nonfiction books on a wide range of subjects, including fashion design, social networking, and body modification. She worked as a DJ at her college radio station during the early years of hip-hop. She makes her home in Seattle, Washington, with her husband and fellow writer, Don Rauf.

## PHOTO CREDITS

Cover Larry Busacca/Getty Images; p. 7 Steve Granitz/WireImage/Getty Images; p. 11 Jason Merritt/TERM/FilmMagic/Getty Images; pp. 12, 43 © AP Images; p. 17 Johnny Nunez/WireImage/Getty Images; p. 19 Getty Images; pp. 21, 36 Chris Polk/FilmMagic/Getty Images; pp. 26, 31 Seth Poppel/Yearbook Library; p. 30 Donaldson Collection/Michael Ochs Archives/Getty Images; p. 33 Vince Bucci/AFP/Getty Images; p. 38 © E! Network/Courtesy: Everett Collection; p. 40 Mike Coppola/FilmMagic/Getty Images; p. 46 Blom/Getty Images; p. 49 Paul Morigi/FilmMagic/Getty Images; p. 51 Jason LaVeris/FilmMagic/Getty Images; p. 53 Dimitrios Kambouris/WireImage/Getty Images; p. 55 Daniel Boczarski/WireImage/Getty Images; p. 62 L. Cohen/WireImage/Getty Images; p. 64 Jeff Kravitz/FilmMagic/Getty Images; p. 70 Karen Minasyan/AFP/Getty Images; p. 72 Drew Angerer/Getty Images; p. 75 Storms Media Group/Alamy Stock Photo; p. 81 Bloomberg/Getty Images; p. 83 Alo Ceballos/GC Images/Getty Images; p. 85 Stringer/AFP/Getty Images; additional interior pages design elements Levchenko Ilia/Shutterstock.com (light streaks), Shmizla/Shutterstock.com (dot pattern), Romeo Budai/EyeEm/Getty Images (sparkle backgrounds).

Design and Layout: Nicole Russo-Duca; Senior Editor: Kathy Kuhtz Campbell; Photo Researcher: Sherri Jackson